Blood Kisses

By Jane Langan

To my Dad, who always said I could.

CONTENTS

Digital

I have made their pictures digital now,
So, when my laptop is left,
Images of my parents and childhood
Spring into technicolour life.

Slideshowing, sweeping across my screen,
Backlit. Places and people.
So many strangers,
Places I don't know.

Who are they, looking at me in twinsets and pearls?
The man in the boat with Mum?
She's laughing, that familiar head thrown back smile
I can almost hear it. Her wavy hair whipped by the wind.

He, with his jumper and strong jaw
Looking straight at camera. Like an old school movie star.
Did my Dad take the photo or someone else?
Who is he?

Out at sea, my Dad didn't travel well.
Only the horizon in view
No life jackets.
Laughing, confidently.

Holding back the rain

I am holding back the rain

    My hands are to my face

        I am holding back the thunder

            The tears are all in place

                I am waiting for the pressure

                To take me

                    Underneath

I am holding back the sun

    My hands shade my eyes

        I am holding back my feelings

        I stroke my arm inside

        I am waiting for the rage

          To take me

            Underneath

I am holding back the storm

    My hands can't stop it now

        I am holding back the shame

            Releasing screams and how

            I am waiting for the peace

          To take me

            Underneath

Moto Heart

Moto moments

Miniscule happenings

Small stuff

Clogging up the

Big cogs

Small blocks

Making shapes

Big bluff

Tick tock

Bump bump

Thump thump

Hello heart

Never noticed

Until stop…

Stop…

Stop.

Plastic Mac Suicide

Plastic mac suicide
What do you know?
Why did she jump?
Nobody knows.

Plastic mac suicide
What do you know?
It ran down her mac,
In runnels so slow

Plastic mac suicide
What do you know?
It couldn't be bloodier,
If she'd slit her wrists…so…

Plastic mac suicide
Smack on the floor
Her body mutilated,
Broken, to the core.

Plastic mac suicide
A splatter and flow
She was more herself then,
Than when she left.

<u>Tattooed Lady</u>

Tattooed lady
Pierced tongue
Mohawk straight
Wearing lace
Not so young
At first look
Make-up took
Lady long time

Tattooed lady
Beginning to fade
No grace just haste
She doesn't get laid
An occasional
Circus freak fuck
Alone in her flat
With her lace, her cat

Tattooed lady
Spent her life
Being different to that
She didn't want
Trouble and strife
A wife's life
How different is this?

Blood Kisses

Blue rinse old lady
Alone in her flat
With her lace, her cat

Outdated

She turned the record over,
the familiar clunk fuzz as the needle
tip toes across the grooves.
Vinyl, jet black spinning,
absorbing light like a black hole.
No dancing or she'll scratch it,
the floorboards bouncing –
It's too late for Purple Rain.
The doves are crying and
Nikki is mast…ing in the
Hot…lob with a zine.
She should replace it,
but it reminds her of her teens.
She binned all the mixtapes,
boyfriends made.
Mostly melted or squirming
like worms pulled from
cassette tapes ejected out of
car stereos too fast.

Alphabet Love

A slow turn,

By the train.

Crying she waved,

'don't go…'

Each minute a year,

Fluctuating between, yes and no?

Hate-Love-Hate.

Indigo madness.

Just deserves,

Keeps the sadness.

Lust. Love undone.

Months, minutes, moments

Nanoseconds, an

Open wound.

Perpetual despairing doom.

Quiet, quiet and still.

Remembering,

Smothering,

Tethered until,

Untied, released,

Venturing into new.

Wandering and wondering,

Xeroxing heart.

Yearning and forgetting.

Zillion tiny pieces. Spreading anew.

Numb

I turn to you in tenderness, you turn in passion,
I offer everything, you feel nothing,
You play with me, I hope for love,
And when you've pulled me apart, you let go.

Oblivion is beautiful,
If you can only find it.
It's a place where minds are numb
And emotion is forgotten.

And now that much time has passed,
I like to think that I am wiser.
But all I really am
Is a skin filled with blood, bones and water.

Cocktail

Bitter twisted, an orange shake.
A cocktail? a vicious turn
For the worse
Is what he called me.

Cynically removed with bite
No life, cold as ice
A frosted over slice of strife,
Is what he called me.

Knife in the gizzard, a gruesome drink,
Which left me over the kitchen sink.
Your puke, you disgusting stench,
Is what he called me.

He, like cheap cider,
The bubbles sparkle, kinda nice.
He is broken spice,
Again, he slaps my face, calls me bitch.

That's the last thing he called me.

The Hill of Shame

Pink and blue

Satin and silk

Here I am at my mother's milk

Full of pain, full of guilt

Full of fear, full of tears

How I wish I was young again.

The darkness of this sordid crime

Of lovers gone, a dirty shrine

Only the love of money made me stay

Only the love of milk and honey

And ambrosia on the hill of shame

How I wish I was young again

Apple sauce and banana skins

Dribble down my Winston's chin

Dull and greying

Like an old wives saying

Or siren singing

How I wish I was young again

The feel of sealing wax

Slowly dripping upon the tax

Dribble and drabble, blending one

As rates and bills go and come

Get paid and again we go

How I wish I was young again

Parchment skin and wills all done
Feelings felt, thoughts begun
The dust, the shit, the bleeding sun
Make me wish that I was young
How I wish I was young again.

Tickity Tock Clock

Time moves us, tick tock.

The clock doesn't stop.

Taxes and death no matter

What.

What?

Time moves us, my skins getting thin.

My clock, biological or not?

Stops or

What.

What?

Time moves us, my hair is grey.

I can't just say, I'm grumpy and hot.

What.

What?

Time moves me, my children are grown.

My seeds are sown.

My future is gone and the past.

Is left, a bit deaf,

What?

What?

You're my Bitch – Or an Ode to Depression

Like the sun you're always there.
Like a friend with a gun, you just don't care.
Like the worst pun, or an unholy nun,
You're a bitch and a dare.

You're the stream that turns to flood.
You're the thoughts that make mind-mud.
You're the babbling brook in my head.
You're a bitch and a dare.

I stilled you, I calmed you
I took you down.
With Prozac and talking
And fulsome purloining.

You took my years and years and years
You aged me, afraid me and made me.

But now I dare you
Try to get in.
You're not on the list.
You're wearing trainers.
You're obviously pissed.

You're my bitch.
You won't be missed.
You're my bitch.

The Song of the Broken Heart

Deep inside the crevices of the broken heart,
there is cracked glass and darkness.
Not a single chink of light,
just the bass thumping, jumping, a tattoo.
The rhythm of the broken heart.

In the mirror, the face skewed in despair.
Looks at eyes filled, red-ringed.
Mascara leaves slug trails,
Along rosacea skin, mouth wet,
nose dribbling. A low-pitched wail, the chord
The music of the broken heart.

The sudden empty bed.
Turning whirring, mind tickling sleep.
Drifting in and out, but the cacophony
of acoustic twangs, strum and tinker
the ache, the insomnia.
The twang, the chord, the bass.
The song of the broken heart.

My Toes are Stout

My eyes are tired
My legs are fat
My belly wobbles
My boobs lie flat

My arms are bingo-winged
My bum sticks out
My fingers arthritic
My toes stout

My hair is grey
My nails crack
My cellulite has cellulite
My stretch marks, stacked

My hips have rhythm
My back has fat
My jowls jiggle
My knees snap

My smile has gone
My lines are maps
My chin jiggles
My face flaps

Home

When I went home
it was to the hills.

Rumbling and tumbling
green and brown.

A quilt of texture
heather and gorse.

Wild grasses blowing
The ashes of my father.

To the westerly wind
Long Mynd.

In glinting evening light
a kestrel overhead eyes prey.

Dipping and rising with the thermal
the very tops of the world.

Home.

Inhibitors

Mood inhibitors
Smoothing collaborators
Vitriolic contaminators
Shiny bright
But not new
Old, worm like
Brass statue
Touched much
Sunlight shows the hue
Mood inhibitors
Cold facilitators
Take you through

Incineration

At the bottom of a black bin, fat tin,
burning so hot, so hot no flames, to tame,
burning all the same, mixed and shredded.
Ashes.

Like the old, crumbling outside, tired bones, inside
passing through purple curtains,
but the swan song is sung, and the mourning has begun.
Slow.

Not so, canned and packed, sour meat bleeding,
ceremony discontinued, like a soap opera slot
sucked out, pressed in, sent off.
Forgot.

At the bottom of a black bin, fat tin,
no bones, blood and muscle unformed.
Not born.
No coffins, that small,
no room for headstones, or grief,
the valley of death out of reach.

SHE/HE

I am HE

HE is you

You is HE

I am lost

Lost are you

You is lost

Lost is too

HE is I

I is SHE

SHE is it

It is me

All is lost

Lost is SHE

Giggle me

Giggle me timbers
A pirate's life for me
Off to the high seas
With a slap of my knee.

That's panto?
I'm Buttons or the prince
A girl in boys clothing
The missing link.

Everything is Fine

'Fuck the world!'
Bad scientist say,
I'm sweet.
Big Corp pays.
I can lie…
in my bed and sleep,
dreaming of dollars
and deceit.
I don't care,
if the pollinators drop
from the sky
on the crops
paralysed and dead
in the fields.
I don't give a…
My moneys in my pocket.
My life rocks.
One small lie
Neonics are harmless.
Everything is fine.

Hands Before Eyes

Hands before eyes
Into bag
Split carton
Yoghurt cherry delight
Under nails
Stained sleeves
Pink glorious
Not what you need

.

Hands before eyes
Into pocket
A lid loose on Lypsyl
A greasy unwelcome
Not on lips
On fingertips
Curious digits
Take more care
Hands before eyes
Adventurers fair

Cucumber

Mind swirls fill the air above,
your head puffs, whilst thinking of salad,
in clouds and water
precipitating pit pat splosh!
Below, up turned umbrellas
ready to catch the drips like
saucers full of milk.
Cats try to return the umbrellas to hemispherical
correctness because they hate
up turned umbrellas and cucumbers most.
We've all seen the social media clips –
The cat's fur, up ended on tip toes, back arched,
escaping their nemesis – sideways.
The cucumber - the worst kind of foe.

My Mothers' Hand's

My mothers' hand's,

Are rough and ingrained with dirt.

Her hands are of the earth.

Planting and pulling up weeds,

and vegetables.

She is constant, outside, hair blowing in the breeze.

My mothers' hand's

Are the last photograph I took of her,

holding a skeleton leaf, she shows my daughter.

Now, her hands are soft, her nails are clean.

Her last journey, out of ambulance, to home.

She, of morphine. Does she see, feel, the outside air?
In bed, in dining room,
I hold her hand, whilst she watches her last sun set,
Her touch is smooth, like new, for her last breath.

Forgot

He didn't forget his manners,
the nurses claimed.
He couldn't remember a name.
But a gentleman, to the end.

He didn't forget his Mum,
Or the mischief he made.
Climbing through windows, late
to avoid his Dad's tirade.

He didn't forget me,
I was there with him,
as much as I could be.
His darling girl. I remained
And he was, always he.

He definitely forgot,
his serious job
where he helped a lot.
The same job all his life.
Forgot.

He definitely forgot,
his wife, fifty-six years wed
until she died.
Then he declined.

Forgot.

He definitely forgot,
the honey,
he had left on a shelf
in the pantry, from home.
Forgot.

He definitely forgot,
How to eat, in the end
Then breathe.
Then be.

But he,
Will never be,
forgot.

A.A. Milne has some explaining to do

A.A. Milne has some explaining to do.
Where is the Hundred Acre Wood, where is Pooh?
I have been looking for Eeyore,
I'm concerned about his mental health.
And as for Tigger, well, he's something else.

I sometimes see Owl but he's no help.
As for Kanga and Roo, they belong in a zoo.
I worry that Pooh may have diabetes, type two.
Honey is healing, but a diet of just that,
Leads to sticky paws, stuck in jars, oh Pooh.

Poor Piglet, so small and sad.
Where is your Mum and Dad? Perhaps he's adopted.
But by whom? Fingers crossed it's not Pooh.
Mind you, that explains why he has to eat haycorns.
And has no trousers at all.

Speaking of pants and bottom half clothes
Are all bears bottoms bare, it must be awfully cold?
 Kanga in her apron and nothing on Roo
As for Tigger, well he is quite nude!

Poor Piglet don't over think it, your scarf will do.

So, A.A Milne what are we to do?

When I was small, I didn't care about

Half-naked bears and animals that belong in a zoo.

Or dysfunctional donkeys, and diabetic Pooh.

I was happy in the Hundred Acre Wood with Christopher Robin,

Thank you.

A small poem for Lola

Soft soft go

Float float no

Giggle giggle blow

And then the sink burped

My Daughters

I don't write about my daughters,
They're curious and bright.
They inspire my poems.
They make dark days light.
They stop me slipping into
A world of self-reverie.

I don't write about my daughters,
Their stars shine, fires ignite.
They're fresh and new,
The world is in their sights.
What they may do is
Amazing to me
But, Oh my gosh,
I wouldn't want to be,
The person who tries to stop
Their juggernaut of might.

I don't write about my daughters,
How proud I am,
Of their successes.
Creative magical creatures,
I can't believe they grew in me.
Independent fierce impressive.
My daughters, my loves, my totality.

Moon Visit

...and the music plays, and notes become words and words become soniferous joy beyond all, even in the quiet places between all the noise and the fullness of Time which tick tocks fatly, wholesome and round in space circling moons and stars, flying, defying its size through the vacuum, not feeling the cold until finally Time chimes midnight...and the owl hoots its tattoo, and the mouse reappears from inside the clock with a large piece of cheese it stole from the waning moon...

White Vans

The white vans
Travel relentlessly around,
My suburban kingdom.
Carrying packages of want
And need for all the people,
Trapped in their houses.

The white vans
With drivers endlessly
On rounds, late and hasty.
Chucking boxes in porches
And playing knock-door-run
With expectant consumers.

The white vans
Filled with cardboard and greed.
Laptop warriors fulfilling their need.
Trapped in a circle of buy-
More-get-more-shop-more-
buy-more indulgent insatiability.

The white vans
Chariots of materialism.
Driven by zero-hour contracts.
Who can't afford a single thing,
Inside their glory hole of
Acquisition.

Blood kisses

He pushes me, shoves me, a punch and a slap.

I'm Judy, a puppet, no control, not intact.

He loves me, he loves me, charming and true.

He's devout at my altar, Hallelujah.

But then the lout is back.

Rusted iron, warmth rolls out of my mouth.

Blood kisses, his sticky hand clutching my face.

Sex pushed hard, face first, into a place.

Paint peeling, then smack….stars…

Then the smell, of my kitchen floor, marred.

'clean up your mess!'

He loves me, '*forgive me*,' he says.

His rage is ferocious, a rising red mist,

like Typhon he muscles and hustles, let's rip.

Lighter burns sizzle on my sausage skin,

He's sinning, he's winning, I'm shattered

like glass, shards in my shin, he throws tins.

Grazes my face, blood ingrained carpet.

My arms, his fingerprints, my legs tread, imprint

'You're stupid fat and ugly.' He mutters in my ear.

'Forgive me, forgive me.'

Home early.

He's fucking, I know that face,

some woman, no grace.

Turns out, I'm Fury, a Banshee, Medusa and more.

Time stops as I whisper, *'get off my floor.'*

Now he's begging, and pleading,

I look at him like he's something I spat.

He's here cos I let him, not gonna listen to his crap.

'You fucked it, dickhead, you tosser, you twat,

I want my home, my money, my life, back.'

<u>No Mercy</u>

There are no more words in me.
They were there; when
my hair, flowed.
My moods and boobs,
Faced up
My head, ached.
Late nights were great.
My body was lean.
My tongue wagged.
My lips and hips kissed.
I yearned and gurned.
I popped and could eat cake.
I had a stash, got mashed.
And I showed.
No Mercy

There are no more words in me.
They're not there; because,
I can't eat cake.
My moods and boobs,
Face down.
My tongue schtum.
My lips and hips cracked.
My head still aches.
I pop painkillers.
Indigestion tablets
And self-medicate.

Blood Kisses

My body is soft.
And my hair knows.
No Mercy

Chemo

Like tiny fish hooks on my skin, licking, licking.

Stop.

I know, you're hungry, I'll get up in a minute, just one more minute.

Let's wait for the nausea to pass. Purrs vibrate through my chest, or lack of it.

Now.

OK enough, get off me. Get down, I can't right now, my head burns.

Head back, eyes closed, galaxies explode in the blackness, too bright, I open them again.

I love you, but please stop licking me, the brine from my eyes encouraging him more.

My hands go to my head. Handfuls of hair free fall.

Gus

He comes in smelling of outside,
wind and dirt in fur.

Wild eyed, feral,
adventures you'll never know.

His 'hello', he's back.
Pet, tame and warm.

Jumping on my lap.
Purring his tattoo.

Blood Kisses

His eyes close as fingers find chin.
Deep in contentment.

Upside down ragdoll black
A hum of tummy rubs, top to tip of tail.

Soft strokes, fingers inch on skin
only at his will.

He is, after all, cat.
Temperament; feisty.

Relaxed then full of fight.
Claws and teeth.

Lashing out, for nowt.
A scratch, pops of blood, on skin.

Like a drunk, no rhyme nor reason.
Just cat.

Not tame, not soft, a stranger.
A wild and feral thing.

Always Summer

I only remember running everywhere,

or skipping.

Or riding my bike.

I occasionally sat,

fidgeting, with grubby fingers,

from misadventures,

getting told off.

Caramelized rice pudding with a dark skin

tasted like heaven at grannie's house.

Sugar sandwiches and oranges peeled for me.

The basement with the mangle

'It'll take your fingers off!'

And Mr. Beauregard the gardener,

always in the roses,

or mowing the lawn.

Was it always summer?

A Skin of Stories

A skin of stories
Of tales gone
And tales to come
Of those loved
And those lost
Of remembered things
And party days
Of calm and hail
Of rain and fun
A drawn-out life
A sum
Of all I am
And will be
A skin of stories
My story. Me.

<u>Changeling</u>

In nineteen seventy-five,
I lost me
I lost me
And there was no
Return.

Changeling forever,
Inside reading it away
Making the words
The sticking plaster
To save the day.

The others didn't see it,
I hid it well, auf and all
Blackened heart
Fairy wings tucked in
Human skin.

The only possible reason
For the hurt
No one could see me
Beneath the pages
The poets slur.

At death, the wraith disappears
Your original
Is washed clean of sin

The golem removed

A child again.

<u>Cocoon</u>

The bass

Reverberates

Through me.

DJ in control.

A tickle of sweat.

I sit then stand

The rush.

My eyes dilate.

Light trails…

Nausea to euphoria…

As I become one…

With bass.

I am dancing.

My teeth clench.

I am the…

Music.

Heaving bodies…

Rhythm…

I feel the air.

I can taste it.

It feels good.

Tuuuuuuuuuune.

My fingers…

Comets…

So bright…

Hugs and

Love…

This place.

A cocoon…

Of bass.

Cold Knees

Cold knees ache
Against ornate tiles
As sun fails to
Shine through hard
Stained glass.
Christ weeps on his cross
With nails through hands and feet.
You wonder, did his feet hurt?
Like your knees?
You wait for the bolt.
BLASPHEMY!
Nail through hands and feet, agony
Statues recreated
A semi-naked tortured man
A symbol of belief
Gazed on by innocent eyes
As thorns pierce his head
A confusion of feelings
A tragic misrepresentation
a myth
A manmade son of god
by manmade words
A manmade religion
A manmade church

Awake

Tumbled duvet
Twisted sheets
Hot mess sweating
Flushing glow
Awake, Awake, Awake.

Punching pillows
Sticky hair
Avoid breathing
Hot breaths
Awake, Awake, Awake.

Angry crying
Crying sleep
Crowded nightmares
Covers off, cold shoulder
Awake, Awake, Awake.

Beside Me

And over pale skies,

clouds like grey collared doves

undulate and surge in breezes,

beyond our whispered touch.

I watch silhouetted birds

move with grace and freedom,

transported by thermals,

rising and falling,

rising and falling.

I think of you,

I think of you...

Beside me when

thunder came.

Beside me when

we wept, over the lost.

We had so much to give,

instead, our insides, turned out.

Beside me when,

joy filled us up,

like chips at the seaside,

whipped in salty air.

Waves of laughter,

heard through the pull of the tide,

rising and falling,

rising and falling.

As we watched pure

happiness seep from every pore,

of those things we made,

unearthly, almost, in their beauty,

luminous in evening light.

You were there, beside me.

ABOUT THE AUTHOR

Jane Langan has poems published in the anthology, Footprints and Echoes. She has been shortlisted in several competitions and had numerous poems published in magazines. Jane has an MA in Creative Writing.

Jane has a successful blog www.howilikemycoffee.blogspot where she has documented her events in her life for over eleven years and is on social media as @MuddyNoSugar and is an editor at Makarelle.com.

Printed in Great Britain
by Amazon